Dear Parent:
Your child's love of reading starts here!

Every child learns to read in a different way and at his or her own speed. Some go back and forth between reading levels and read favorite books again and again. Others read through each level in order. You can help your young reader improve and become more confident by encouraging his or her own interests and abilities. From books your child reads with you to the first books he or she reads alone, there are I Can Read Books for every stage of reading:

SHARED READING
Basic language, word repetition, and whimsical illustrations, ideal for sharing with your emergent reader

BEGINNING READING
Short sentences, familiar words, and simple concepts for children eager to read on their own

READING WITH HELP
Engaging stories, longer sentences, and language play for developing readers

READING ALONE
Complex plots, challenging vocabulary, and high-interest topics for the independent reader

ADVANCED READING
Short paragraphs, chapters, and exciting themes for the perfect bridge to chapter books

I Can Read Books have introduced children to the joy of reading since 1957. Featuring award-winning authors and illustrators and a fabulous cast of beloved characters, I Can Read Books set the standard for beginning readers.

A lifetime of discovery begins with the magical words **"I Can Read!"**

Visit www.icanread.com for information
on enriching your child's reading experience.

Paddington Sets Sail Text copyright © 2016 by Michael Bond. Story adapted by Christy Webster from an original Paddington story written by Michael Bond. Illustrations copyright © 2016 by HarperCollins Publishers. All rights reserved. Manufactured in China. No part of this book may be used or reproduced in any manner whatsoever without written permission except in the case of brief quotations embodied in critical articles and reviews. For information address HarperCollins Children's Books, a division of HarperCollins Publishers, 195 Broadway, New York, NY 10007.
www.icanread.com

Library of Congress Control Number: 2015950811
ISBN 978-0-06-243065-6 (trade bdg.) — ISBN 978-0-06-243064-9 (pbk.)

Typography by Rick Farley

16 17 18 19 20 SCP 10 9 8 7 6 5 4 3 2 1   ❖   First Edition

I Can Read!

BEGINNING 1 READING

PADDINGTON
Sets Sail

Michael Bond
illustrated by R. W. Alley

HARPER
An Imprint of HarperCollinsPublishers

One morning,

Mr. Brown had a surprise.

"We're taking a trip

to the beach!" he said.

Paddington, Jonathan, and Judy

cheered.

Mrs. Brown and Mrs. Bird
were excited, too.

Paddington had never been
to the beach.
He did not know what to bring,
so he packed everything.

Soon they were on their way.

Paddington poked his head

out the window.

He sniffed the salty sea air.

At the beach,
Paddington got a pail, shovel,
sunglasses, and a float.

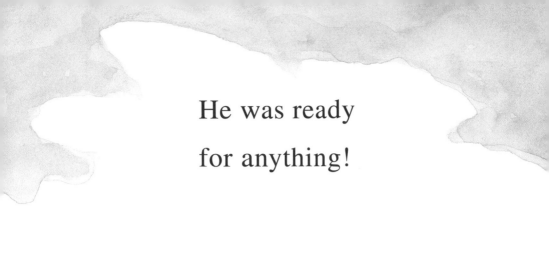

He was ready

for anything!

The tide was low,

so they went in the water.

Jonathan and Judy

splashed and swam.

Paddington floated in the waves.

At lunch,

Mr. Brown had a great idea.

He said, "Let's have

a sand castle contest!"

12

Paddington, Judy, and Jonathan
would each make a sand castle.
The biggest castle would win.

Paddington wanted to win.

First, he found a perfect spot.

He dug a moat.

He carried

pails and pails of sand.

He made walls and windows.

15

Paddington placed his hat
on top of the castle.
Finally, he was done.
Paddington's big sand castle
was perfect!

Paddington sat
inside his castle.
Sand castle work was hard
and he was tired.

Then he fell asleep.

Oh no!

The tide had come in!

It knocked down

Paddington's sand castle.

It carried Paddington's pail

out to sea—

with Paddington in it!

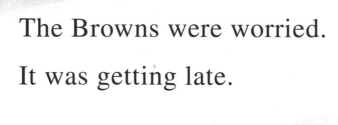

The Browns were worried.

It was getting late.

They found Paddington's hat
but could not find Paddington.
Where had he gone?

Then the Browns spotted

people gathered

near the pier.

They ran toward the crowd.

It was Paddington!

People believed
that Paddington had floated
all the way across the sea.
They took his picture.

"Did you float here in this pail?"
a girl asked.

"Yes. I used my shovel
as a paddle," said Paddington.

The sun was setting.

It was time to go home.

"Did you enjoy your trip,

Paddington?" asked Judy.

"Yes. Not many bears go to sea

in a bucket," he said.

The Browns were so happy
to have Paddington back.
"Today's trip was a bit shorter
than when you came
from Darkest Peru,"
said Mr. Brown.

BRIGHTSEA →
2 m

Paddington did not hear.

He was fast asleep.